MAD DOGS
AND
ENGLISHMEN

... go out in the midday sun.

Ian Collis

Introduction

'Mad dogs and Englishman go out in the midday sun' ... so sang the great composer Noel Coward about the game of cricket, which has been played on various pitches around the world. It is a good time then, in this new millennium, to take a look back at the game of cricket and to see how these 'Mad dogs and Englishmen' – and everyone in between – have produced not only some of the game's finest moments, but also some very quirky and unusual images.

After gaining a foothold in the public consciousness, the game of cricket was introduced into the colonies in the 1800s and became a means of identifying with the British Empire. As England put her stamp on the world, some of the best of British traditions were transferred in the game of cricket. Although the first international cricket match was actually between the USA and Canada in 1844, the English touring team to Australia in 1877 saw the official birth of Test cricket. The Australians then toured England the following year and a tradition was born ... the Ashes!

By 1889, South Africa became the third Test nation. The following year the official English County Championships was formed, Australia started the Sheffield Shield competition in 1892–93, followed by the Currie Cup in South Africa, the Plunkett Shield in New Zealand and the Ranji Trophy in India. The game was reaching around the world and through its popularity with players and the public, cricket matches were played in the true spirit of sportsmanship.

The period between1890 and the outbreak of WW1 has since been known as The Golden Age of Cricket with names such as W.G.Grace, Victor Trumper, Wilfred Rhodes, C.B.Fry and K.S.Ranjitsinhji featuring prominently. The ICC (Imperial Cricket Conference) was formed in 1909 with England, Australia and South Africa followed by the inclusion of

India, West Indies and New Zealand prior to World War II, and Pakistan, shortly afterwards. By the end of the 20th Century Sri Lanka, Zimbabwe and Bangladesh were also given Test status.

The game has had its challenges, such as the 'Bodyline' series of 1932–33, the suspension of South Africa from 1970–1991 because of apartheid policies, and the advent of World Series Cricket in 1977, but there have always been those lighter moments. This book captures many of them … the great games, the memorable teams, the champion players, the unusual characters, challenging playing conditions, the famous grounds, the large crowds, the birth of night cricket, the limited overs revolution, increased media scrutiny, the introduction of new technology and many, many more.

There have been countless books written, photos published and statistics gathered on the game of cricket. This book tries a different approach in trying to capture the rare and the unusual … the 'ghost' of W.G. Grace; the deeds of Don Bradman and the other great names of the game; the overseas tours with various fashions at play; the huge crowds walking onto the field during the lunch break; the famous scoreboards, many now long gone; the pre-television era when a picture was worth a thousand words; the timeless Tests and players victorious cheered off the ground through a guard of honour and, of course, the ever-changing and volatile English summer.

This amazing collection of rare photos shows the games in all its glory and in many different eras. Complete with captions and essential trivia, this is the ideal gift book for the cricket fan, the budding historian or for those who love nostalgia.

I hope you will enjoy 'Mad Dogs and Englishmen' – and everyone in between.

Ian Collis, September 2015.

Lords is always a great sight, especially when England and Australia do battle in a Test match, as was this occasion in 1905 when all vantage points were taken.

There have been tens of thousands of cricket days such as this … a small picturesque ground, the sound of leather on willow splitting the quiet surrounds. A day enjoyed by 'Mad Dogs and Englishmen' and everyone in between.

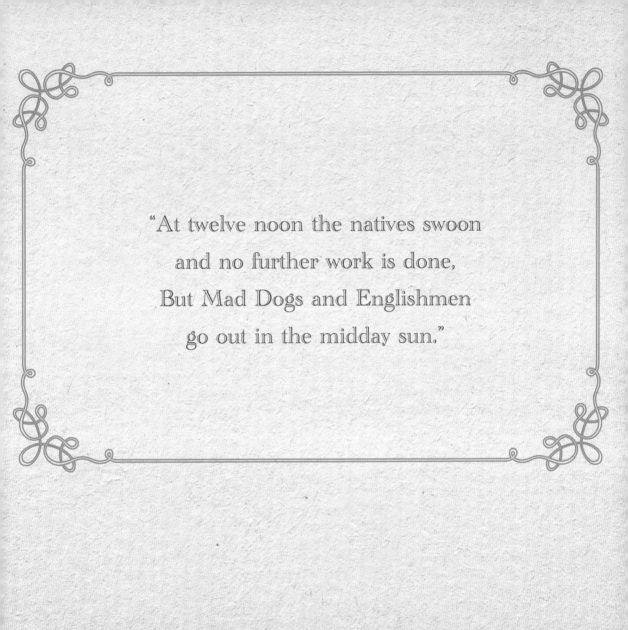

"At twelve noon the natives swoon
and no further work is done,
But Mad Dogs and Englishmen
go out in the midday sun."

The English touring team that started the international rivalry in 1876.

The Australian XI in England in 1880. A century before the 'pyjama game' took cricket by storm, the Aussies look resplendent in their tour gear, with G.J.Bonnor (middle in the back row) a veritable giant. Captained by W.L.Murdoch (seated third from the left) the team played just nine first-class matches, which included one Test match, the first ever played on English soil.

Australian greats of a bygone era … Murdoch, Spofforth, Boyle and Bannerman. Billy Murdoch, captain of the 1880, 1882 and 1884 Australian teams, passed away suddenly when he was a spectator at the Australia v South Africa Test in Melbourne in 1911. Murdoch seized with apoplexy during the lunch break and died later in the afternoon. Fred 'The Demon' Spofforth, a larger than life character, was Australia's first true fast bowler. In 18 Tests from 1874 to 1888, he captured 94 wickets at an average of 18.41. Henry Frederick Boyle. On 27 May 1878, Spofforth and Boyle dismissed the MCC for totals of 33 and 19 in one afternoon. After playing for Victoria against the Englishmen in 1873, Boyle often recalled with pride the fact that he bowled W.G. Grace. A.C. Bannerman was a member of five tours to England, from 1880–1893. He was probably the most famous of all the stonewalling batsmen, his patience was said to be inexhaustible.

A male-dominated cricket crowd at the Sydney Cricket Ground, sweltering in their suits in February 1895. With the beer stand keeping the patrons refreshed on this hot summer's day, the scoreboard reflected the home side's complete control of the match … Australia scored 284 against England, 65, and 29 for 5 in their second innings.

The ghost of W.G.Grace shuffles its way from the cricket fields of yesteryear. This wonderful photo, with all its creases and aging, certainly appears to show the great man in ghost form, but his deeds were very much forged by blood and sweat. Grace debuted as a 16-year-old in a first-class match 150 years ago and played for the next 40 years as his reputation grew to extraordinary heights. A fine, almost trim athlete in his younger years, as his waistline grew and his beard became streaked with grey, his reputation and character developed. Grace's batting was a revelation … he pioneered the combination of forward and back play, cleverly using his feet. Timid umpires were no match for this larger than life sportsman. In 1876, he was on just 6 runs when he was given not out to a plumb lbw delivery because, as the umpire later conceded, the large crowd had come to see him play. That day, he went on to score 400 not out. As the players made their way off the field the scorer had Grace on 399, but W.G. advised him to round it up to 400, which he dutifully did.

A cartoon of the period, with W.G.Grace towering over Bobby Abel in the debate about payment of players, and 'amateurs and gentlemen'.

The 'larger than life' figure of W.G.Grace towers over Kumar Ranjitsinhji (left) and William Murdoch (right). Grace played 870 first class matches from 1865–1908, scoring a phenomenal 54,211 runs and taking 2,809 wickets.

Kumar Shri Ranjitsinhji, a member of Andrew Stoddart's 1897 England team, was an Indian prince who was not only a fine batsman, but also brought new strokes to the game. He introduced the late cut and leg glance, as well as the technique of back-foot defence. His first-class career spanned 27 years from 1893–1920, scoring 24,692 runs with a top score of 285 and an enviable average of 56.37.

A caricature of Alfred Lyttelton (1857–1913) which bears a striking resemblance to comedian John Cleese. A British politician who excelled at both cricket and football, Lyttelton was no joke as a wicketkeeper and batsman, although he only appeared in four Tests. At The Oval in 1884, Lyttelton gave the gloves to W.G. Grace and took four Australian wickets with underarm lobs!

Smartly-dressed spectators during the Australia v Kent match at St Lawrence Ground, Canterbury, in 1905. The Australian team is on the right in the foreground as well as in the row behind.

Spectators at a match held at the Crystal Palace, between the Australians and Gentlemen of England, 1899. Pictured are five of the 'Gentlemen' team … W.P.Howell, A.C.McLaren, C.Robson, W.G.Grace, A.Jones and W.Brearley.

The lunch interval during a match between Australian and Sussex at New County Ground, Howe, Brighton in 1899. It was a common occurrence for the spectators to wander across the ground during the breaks for lunch and tea in early days. Although difficult to see, on the scoreboard in the middle of the photo it has Victor Trumper 300 not out, Joe Darling 45 not out and Australia 624 for 4. Trumper had bat for just 380 minutes for his score, belting 36 fours, and it had beaten the previous highest score by an Australian in England.

Joseph Vine had a limited Test career for England, but was one of the most popular Sussex professionals. He appeared in 421 consecutive matches and missed only one match in 503 in a 26-year career from 1896–1922.

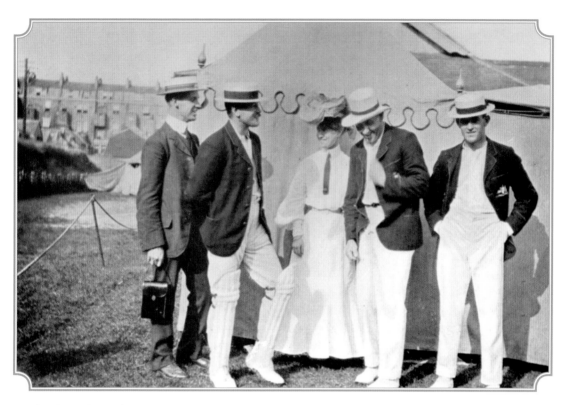

'Did you hear the one about …?' Australians (from left) Philip Newland, Reggie A. Duff, Mrs Jo Newland, D.R. 'Algy' Gehrs and Albert 'Tibby' Cotter share a joke, 1905.

Australians Clem Hill, Hugh Trumble, James Kelly and Victor Trumper stand on the deck of H.M.S. Victory, 1905. The spot where Lord Horatio Nelson fell in the Battle of Trafalgar a century before is marked by a raised inscription in front of Mr Kelly's right foot.

Rival captains in the final game of the 1905 tour at Hastings, Australia's Joe Darling (left) and W.G. Grace. There is no truth to the rumour Grace told his opponent after the toss, 'Alright, you can bat Darling…' (Apologies to Black Adder).

Away from the on-field action, Australia's Frank Laver in a Rover car in England. On the 1905 tour, Laver was appointed player-manager, which explains why he got first use of the tour car.

July 1906, 40 winks not out ... (from left to right) Hammersmith luminaries Councillor R.Green, Mayor T.Chamberlin and Town Clerk W.Thompson, attending a 'Grand Cricket Match' at Hammersmith .... if they could only can stay awake.

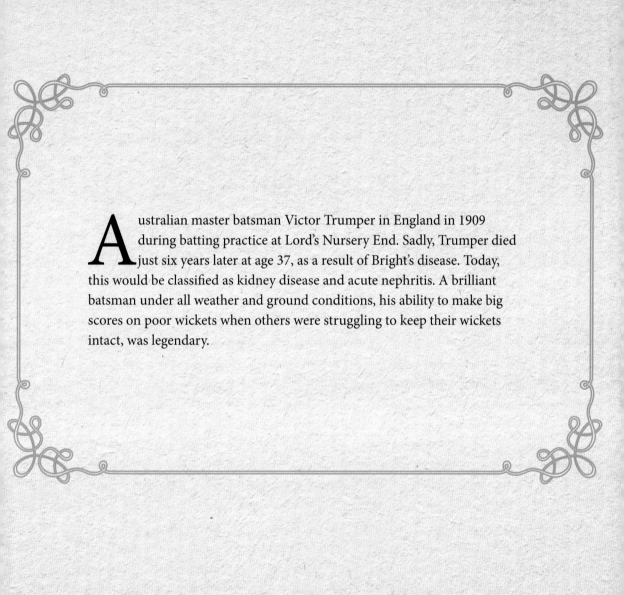

Australian master batsman Victor Trumper in England in 1909 during batting practice at Lord's Nursery End. Sadly, Trumper died just six years later at age 37, as a result of Bright's disease. Today, this would be classified as kidney disease and acute nephritis. A brilliant batsman under all weather and ground conditions, his ability to make big scores on poor wickets when others were struggling to keep their wickets intact, was legendary.

Victor Trumper on tour in Hastings, England, in 1905. Trumper's wife Annie is on the left in a white dress and dark hair as the great man tries out local transport options.

It's formal wear attire only as spectators enter Lord's for the Eton v Harrow cricket match in the 1920s.

Essex and England captain J.W.H.T. Douglas, 1912. An obdurate batsman who was nicknamed 'Johnny Won't Hit Today', a play on his initials given to him by Australian hecklers, his talents were not confined to cricket. He was also a middleweight boxer who became an Olympic champion at the 1908 London Games, defeating Australian Reg 'Snowy' Baker in the final. Douglas captained England at cricket on 18 occasions. A courageous man to the end, he passed away in 1930, aged just 48, when he was drowned at sea trying to save his father's life after two vessels collided in the fog.

Australian Warwick Armstrong, or 'Big Ship' as he was affectionately known, due to his sheer physical size, was a great all-rounder who played 50 Tests from 1902–1921. A huge powerful driving right-hand batsman and fast medium and leg break slow bowler, he was also one of his country's finest ever captains.

Crowds flocked to watch cricket Test matches, especially between Australia and England, at The Oval, 13 August 1921. Lionel Hallam Tennyson moves out to inspect the wicket under police protection, prior to the fifth Test against Australia. Tennyson was the grandson of the famous poet Alfred Lord Tennyson (Poet Laureate of the United Kingdom during much of Queen Victoria's reign).

Arthur Gilligan, captain of the England cricket team in 1924-25. He will always be remembered as one of the most popular and inspiring of England's captains. A right hand batsman and right arm fast-medium bowler. While his Test career was all too brief, his contribution to the game was immense. Even at the height of his career and for many years after retirement he was always promoting the game, either lecturing or speaking at dinners to spread the enthusiasm for the game he loved so much.

The ball that did the trick. Australian cricketer Arthur Mailey holds the ball which dismissed Australia for just 125 runs in the fifth Test match in 1926. The most dangerous Australian spin bowler of the immediate post-war period, Mailey played in a mere 21 Tests from 1920–1926, capturing 99 wickets, which included 36 in the 1920-21 Ashes series.

Nᴼ 1 TOTAL. Nᴼ 3

232 428 0

WICKETS 1

BOWLER 4 **BOWLER** 10
CAUGHT
2 **LAST PLAYER** 1 83

LAST WICKET FELL AT 428

Surrey v Oxford University at The Oval, June 1926. Englishmen Jack Hobbs (left) and Andy Sandham in front of the scoreboard after setting up a record opening partnership of 428.

The brilliant English opening pair of Jack Hobbs (right) and Herbert Sutcliffe share the silverware spoils in Australia 1924–25. The greatest opening pair in Test history, they amassed 3249 runs in 38 innings, with 15 century stands at an overall average of 87.81. While individually they rank as two of the great batsmen in cricket, together they were brilliant. In the final Test of the 1926 Ashes series, Hobbs and Sutcliffe put on 172 for the opening wicket after heavy rain overnight on the uncovered pitch had turned the wicket into a treacherous 'sticky' wicket. This turned the match and the series England's way.

England all-rounder Maurice Tate displays the bowling action that made him a feared wicket-taker in 39 Tests during the 1920s and 1930s.

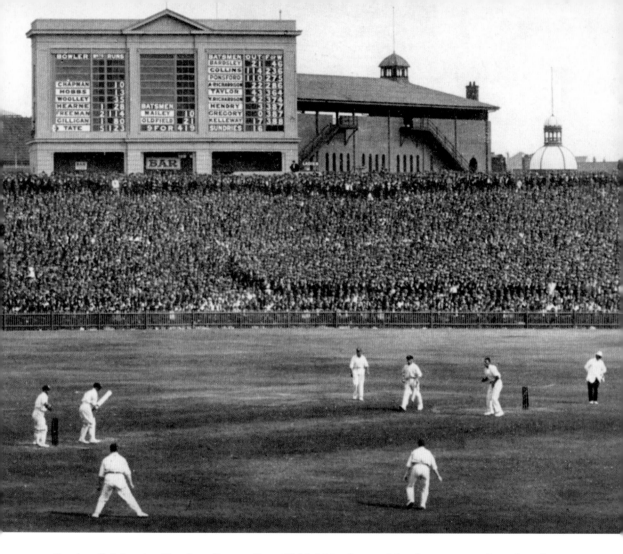

England's Maurice Tate bowling to Bert Oldfield in front of the famous scoreboard at the Sydney Cricket Ground in the 1924 series in front of a packed hill area.

There have been hundreds of non-descript cricket clubs, such as this 'bush league' from Country NSW in the 1920s, in every country that have played the game over the decades. This one, from the Southern Highlands, is special … the young man sitting in the second row, third from the right in a cap is Don Bradman.

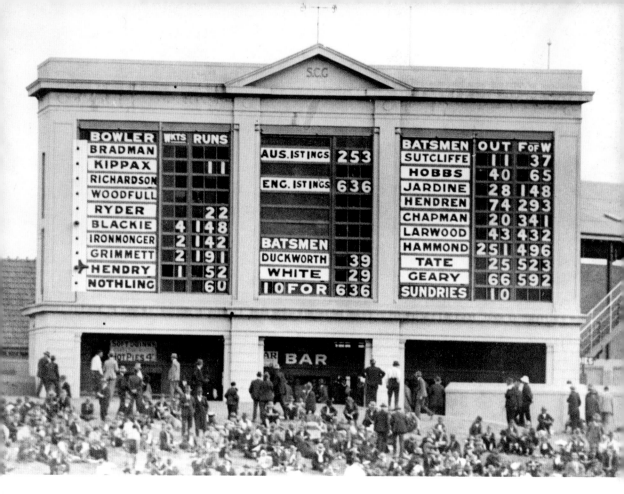

The SCG scoreboard for the second Test between Australia and England in 1928. A.P.F. Chapman's England team dominated the home team, winning the Test series 4–1. In the first Test in Brisbane, England won by a massive 675 runs, which to this day remains the largest winning run margin in a Test between the countries. Nine days later, England put the cleaners through their opponents in Sydney, eventually winning by eight wickets.

Members of the South Africa team try out bats and pads at Stuart Surridge's store after their arrival in England, 1929.

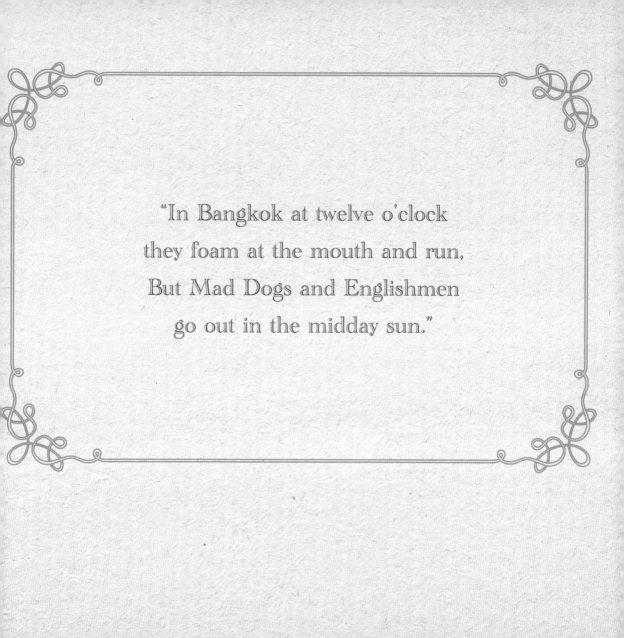

"In Bangkok at twelve o'clock
they foam at the mouth and run,
But Mad Dogs and Englishmen
go out in the midday sun."

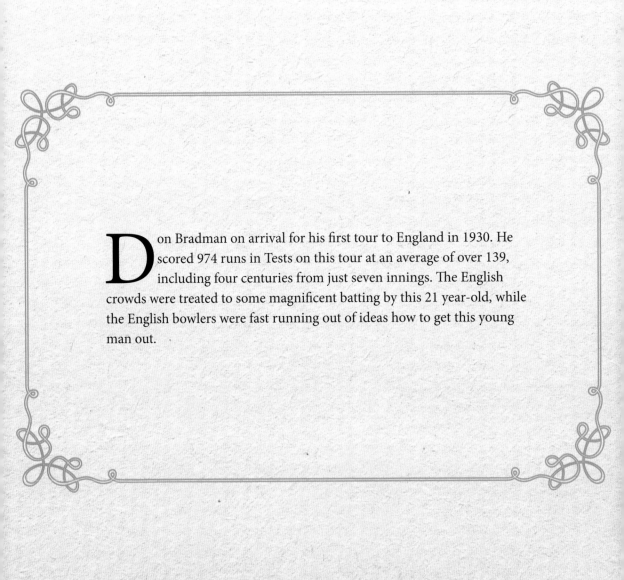

Don Bradman on arrival for his first tour to England in 1930. He scored 974 runs in Tests on this tour at an average of over 139, including four centuries from just seven innings. The English crowds were treated to some magnificent batting by this 21 year-old, while the English bowlers were fast running out of ideas how to get this young man out.

SMOKING 2517 SMOKING 1

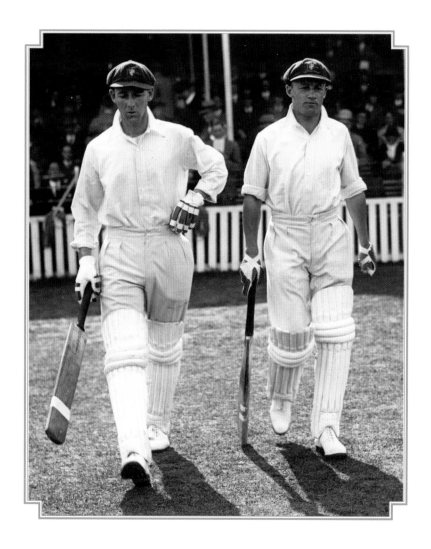

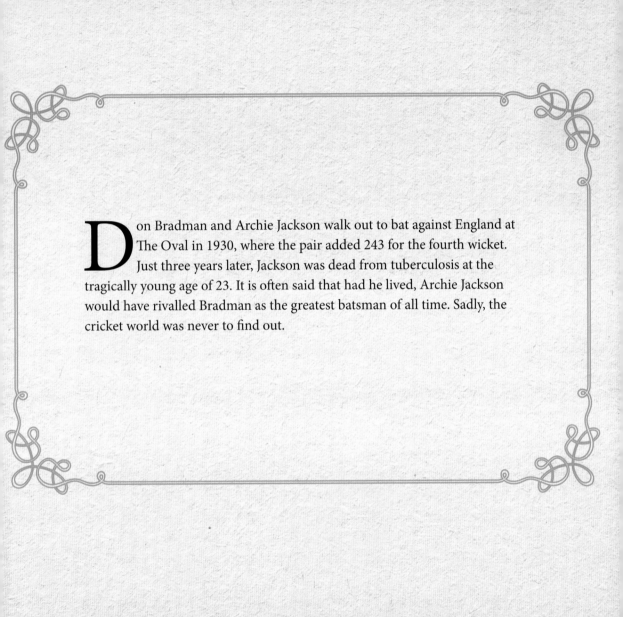

Don Bradman and Archie Jackson walk out to bat against England at The Oval in 1930, where the pair added 243 for the fourth wicket. Just three years later, Jackson was dead from tuberculosis at the tragically young age of 23. It is often said that had he lived, Archie Jackson would have rivalled Bradman as the greatest batsman of all time. Sadly, the cricket world was never to find out.

Fascinating images of the English cricketers enjoying the Sydney Harbour away from the rigours of the infamous Bodyline tour in the summer of 1932–33. Not looking nearly as fearsome as they were on the field, from left to right, are Freddie Brown, Tommy Mitchell (foreground), Leslie Ames (background), Eddie Painter, Wally Hammond and others, with Maurice Leyland in the water in front of the boat.

Back on land after their swim. From left to right, Nawad of Pataudi (smoking the pipe), Harold Larwood, Eddie Paynter (foreground), Wally Hammond (in robe), Maurice Leyland, Leslie Ames and Freddie Brown sitting on the sand. Pataudi was a casualty on the tourists' team when he refused to field at leg side in the second Test. Pataudi was subsequently dropped for the next Test in Melbourne and didn't play on tour again. Douglas Jardine also completely ignored him for the rest of the tour matches. Later Pataudi would comment of Jardine, "I am told he has his good points, but in three months I have yet to see them."

The most hated team in cricket history? Many Australian fans that watched the tactics of Douglas Jardine's MCC team during the infamous 'Bodyline' series of 1932–33 certainly thought so. Jardine earned the ire of cricket lovers when he instructed his fast bowlers to bowl at the leg side of the Australian players – effectively the body – in order to limit the stroke player of star batsman Don Bradman. The ploy worked, and England regained the Ashes, but did not win over many new fans to the game.

LEFT: Rival captains Douglas Jardine and Bill Woodfull walk off the pitch during the controversial 'Bodyline' series of 1932–33. 'Hey, Jardine,' yelled one Australian supporter during the divisive series, 'where's yer butler to carry yer bat for you?'

RIGHT: George Headley, described by many at the time as the 'Bradman of the West Indies' in 1933. Headley scored runs with a style and brilliance, setting the standard for later generations of West Indian players to follow.

The England players watching the Test match intently from the dressing room at Headingley, 1934. The match finished in a draw after Don Bradman scored a record 304 runs in Australia's first innings total of 584.

Spectators enjoy homemade sandwiches during the lunch break in the mammoth Australian score of 701 at The Oval in August 1934. Australia won the match by 562 runs to regain the Ashes.

Groundsman 'Bosser' Martin overseeing the use of the heavy four tonne roller, nicknamed 'Bosser's Pet', prior to the fifth Test at The Oval in 1934.

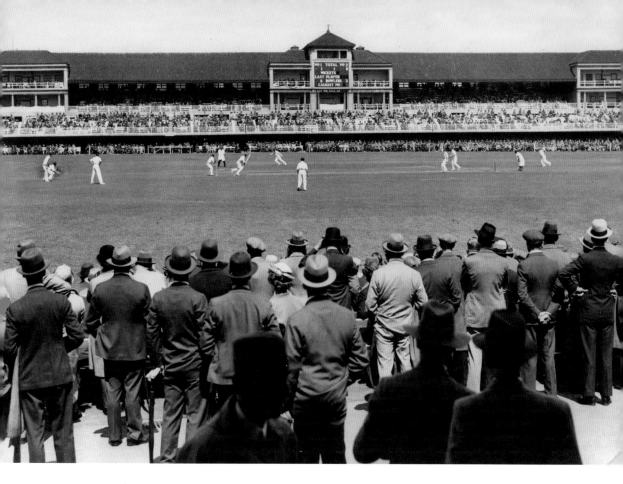

A spectator's perspective at the start of play for the second Test between England and Australia at Lord's in June 1934. England won the Test by an innings and 38 runs to tie the Ashes series with three Tests remaining.

Former England Test captain (1888–89 v South Africa) and Hollywood actor Charles Aubrey Smith (1863–1948) watching the England v Australia Test at Trent Bridge in 1938. Primarily a right arm fast bowler, his unusually curved run-up, starting at deep mid-off, earned him the nickname 'Round the Corner Smith'. On the acting front, his first major role in Hollywood was *The Prisoner of Zenda* (1937). An established character actor, he captained the Hollywood XI which starred fellow actors Errol Flynn, David Niven and Ray Milland.

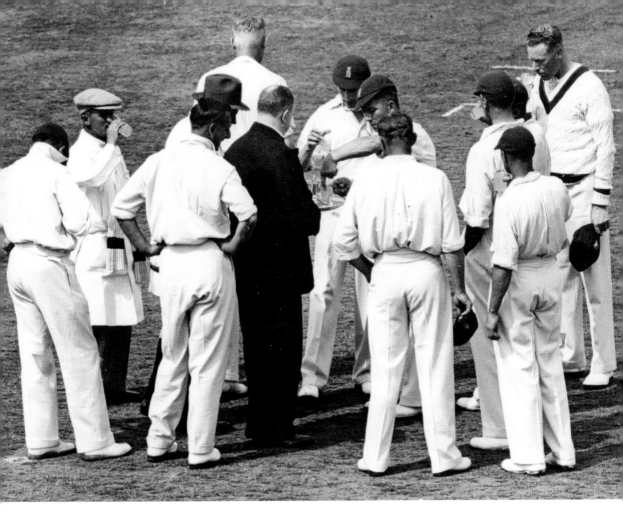

Players and umpires earned their refreshments during the 'timeless' Test match at The Oval in 1934, with an immaculately dressed drinks waiter looking every inch an Englishman's butler.

Don Bradman catching up with his correspondence while resting in his hotel room on tour in England, 1938. 'The Don', as he was widely known, was a keen correspondent with various newspaper publishers and cricket fans back home and around the world. As a piece of memorabilia how much would the 'D.B.' case be worth today? Priceless …

October, 1931.

A series of newspaper posters heralding Don Bradman's batting feats in England in the 1930s.

A series of collectable cigarette cards from the 1938 Ashes series picturing rival captains Bradman and Yardley, and a number of great players from each team.

W. J. EDRICH

K. FARNES

H. GIMBLETT

W. J. O'REILLY

M. G. WAITE

C. W. WALKER

Australian Stan McCabe runs into the pavilion through a corridor of spectators after scoring 232 against England at Trent Bridge in June 1938.

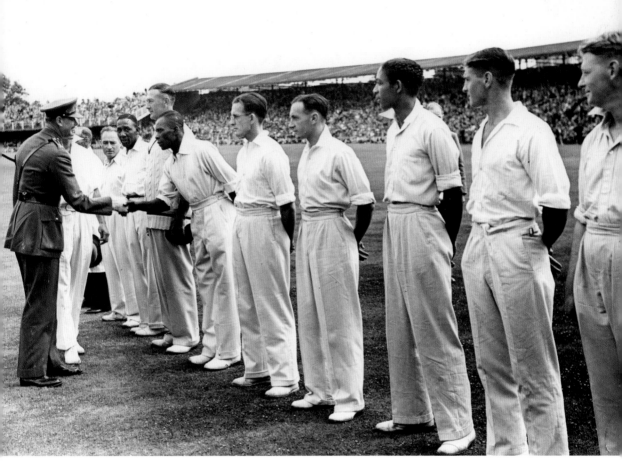

England v the Dominions at Lord's during the war years, in August 1943. England won the toss and the match. The Dominions team were made up of players from Australia, West Indies and South Africa. Future fast bowling great Keith Miller is pictured second from right.

The players hit the ground during the Army v RAF match as bombs land close to the ground at Lord's. In true English spirit, play resumed shortly after.

A tranquil rural setting for a cricket match at Northam, Western Australia, in 1946. So typical of many cricket grounds around the world … the flannelled fools, the mesmerised crowd and the heat!

Somewhere along the Nullarbor Plain, October 1946. At the piano in the saloon car of the transcontinental train is Dick Pollard. The choir (from left to right) are Jack Ikin, Rupert Howard, James Langridge, Peter Smith and Bill Voce.

Rival captains Don Tallon (Australia) and Wally Hammond (England) flip for the toss before a Test on the 1946–47 England Tour of Australia. Note the lack of formality – especially Hammond in civilian hat and cigarette in hand.

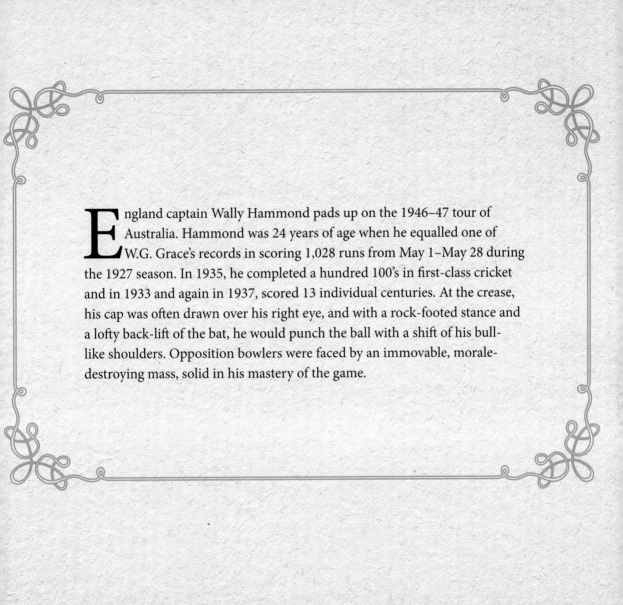

England captain Wally Hammond pads up on the 1946–47 tour of Australia. Hammond was 24 years of age when he equalled one of W.G. Grace's records in scoring 1,028 runs from May 1–May 28 during the 1927 season. In 1935, he completed a hundred 100's in first-class cricket and in 1933 and again in 1937, scored 13 individual centuries. At the crease, his cap was often drawn over his right eye, and with a rock-footed stance and a lofty back-lift of the bat, he would punch the ball with a shift of his bull-like shoulders. Opposition bowlers were faced by an immovable, morale-destroying mass, solid in his mastery of the game.

Is it Ian Fleming or perhaps James Bond? No, it's Denis Compton, England and Middlesex cricketer, as well as Arsenal footballer, signing autographs for fans at the Denis Compton Ball in London in the late 1940s. The ball was the last event of Denis' cricket benefit programme, and was attended by many leading personalities from the worlds of sport and entertainment.

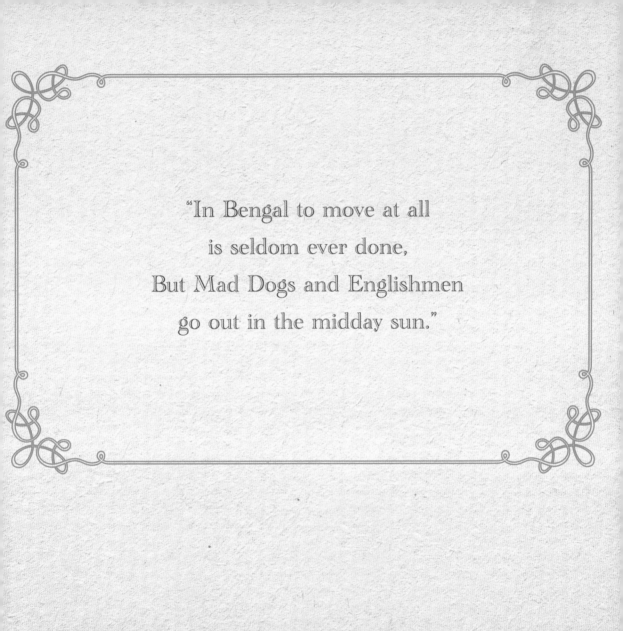

"In Bengal to move at all
is seldom ever done,
But Mad Dogs and Englishmen
go out in the midday sun."

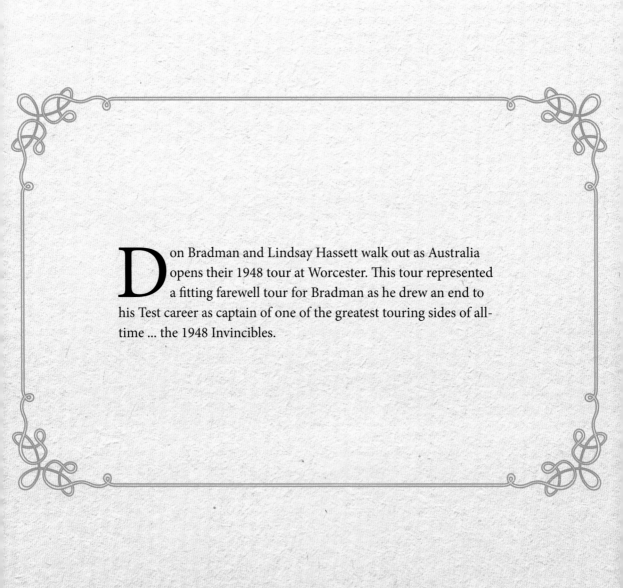

Don Bradman and Lindsay Hassett walk out as Australia opens their 1948 tour at Worcester. This tour represented a fitting farewell tour for Bradman as he drew an end to his Test career as captain of one of the greatest touring sides of all-time ... the 1948 Invincibles.

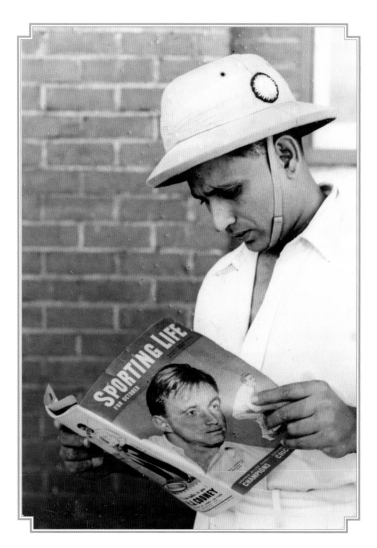

Wearing his characteristic pith helmet Lala Amarnath, captain of the first post-Independence India cricket team, studies Don Bradman's article on captaincy in the October issue of Sporting Life in Australia, 1947–48.

Lala Amarnath at the crease, hits out against Australian slow bowler Colin McCool in January 1948.

England bowler Jim Laker in training at The Oval, 1948. A very different approach to the training methods we have today … 'does this tickle?'

Touring the grounds of Balmoral Castle are members of the 1948 Australia team, who completed their victorious tour by defeating Scotland at Aberdeen. King George V is seen talking to Don Bradman at the front of the group, with Queen Elizabeth (later the Queen Mother) behind them.

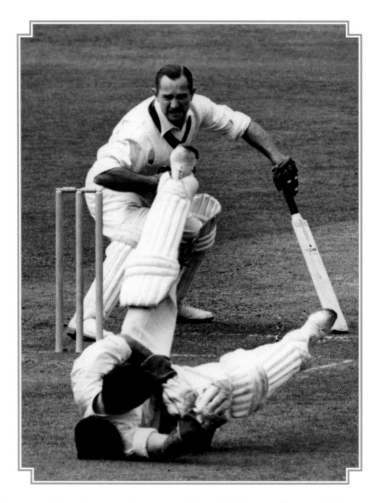

Godfrey Evans, a wicket-keeping law unto himself, brings off one of his countless brilliant catches to dismiss Sid Barnes at Nottingham in 1948.

The crowd within, the crowd without. England v Australia, Leeds 1948. Australia won the fourth Test to regain the Ashes.

Above left: Catching the action, 1948 style. Closely following the play and ready to photograph the action with a 'long tom' camera, our photographer finds a good viewpoint on the score-box roof.

Above right: The first stage in the journey is getting the negatives to the newspaper offices. A photographer lowering exposed plates in a sack to a messenger from the score-box roof.

Opposite top: An important link in the organisation. A corner of the temporary depot established near the cricket ground, where the photographic plates are developed and printed before being rushed to London and the provincial newspapers.

Opposite bottom: Sighted to cover phases of the play away from the wickets, a 30-inch camera is positioned on the pavilion roof with a messenger boy waiting for the exposed plate.

The English team give three rousing cheers for Australia's captain Don Bradman when he came to the crease in the final Test at The Oval during the 1948 tour. Norman Yardley (centre) raises his cap as he leads the applause for Bradman (right) as he walked out to the crease.

Bradman is bowled second ball for a duck by spin bowler Eric Hollies. Bradman came to the crease with a batting average of 101.39 and needed only 4 runs to retire on a 100+ Test career average. As it was, he was stranded on 99.94.

Don Bradman ends his Test career in triumph. From the balcony of the grandstand at The Oval, England captain Norman Yardley calls for three cheers for 'The Don'. 'This is rather a sad occasion for me,' Bradman told the crowd who had gathered in front of the pavilion. 'Whatever you may have read to the contrary, this is definitely the last Test match in which I shall ever play.'

CRICKET
— 1948 – Australian Team in England —

BATTING

	L	NO	RS	AGG.	AV.
BRADMAN D.G.	31	4	187	2428	89·92
HASSETT A.L.	27	6	200*	1563	74·42
MORRIS A.R.	29	2	290	1922	71·18
BROWN W.A.	26	1	200	1448	57·92
LOXTON S.	22	5	159*	973	57·23
BARNES S.G.	27	3	176	1354	56·41
HARVEY N.R.	27	6	126	1129	53·76
MILLER K.R.	26	3	202*	1088	47·30
HAMENCE R.A.	22	4	99	582	32·33
JOHNSON I.W.	22	4	113*	543	30·16
TALLON D.	13	2	53	283	25·72
LINDWALL R.R.	20	3	77	411	24·17
SAGGERS R.	12	3	104*	209	23·22
McCOOL C.L.	18	3	76	306	20·40
JOHNSTON W.A.	18	8	29	188	18·80
RING D.	14	5	53	150	16·66
TOSHACK E.R.	12	3	20*	78	8·66
Sundries					

BOWLING

	O.	M.	R.	W.	AV.
LINDWALL R.R.	573	139	1358	86	15·79
JOHNSTON W.A.	850	279	1699	102	16·65
MILLER K.R.	429	117	992	56	17·71
McCOOL C.L.	399	98	1018	57	17·85
JOHNSON I.W.	668	228	1069	57	18·37
TOSHACK E.R.	502	171	1069	50	21·38
HAMENCE R.A.	56	13	151	7	21·57
LOXTON S.	361	91	704	32	22·15
RING D.	542	155	1328	60	22·13

COPYRIGHT APPLIED FOR

ALSO BOWLED (First Class Matches)

	O.	M.	R.	W.	AV.
BROWN	4	0	16	4	4·00
HARVEY	10	2	29	1	29·00
MORRIS	9	1	91	1	
BARNES	65	16	121	2	60·50
HASSETT	12	0	48	0	
BRADMAN	1	0	2	0	

Compiled & Drawn by C.A.Kable

The tour card of the 1948 Invincibles … Bradman's unbeaten Australian team in England.

RIGHT: In 1948 English crowds could not get enough of the brilliant Australian tourists. Part of the huge crowd, which packed The Oval for Don Bradman's final Test appearance.

England batsman Denis Compton reels away holding his face after playing on a rising ball from Australian fast bowler Ray Lindwall in the third Test at Manchester, 1948.

ABOVE LEFT: Members of the Australian team assist Denis Compton from the field after his unlucky injury. On Compton's left is Ian Johnson; walking behind with Compton's bat is Don Bradman. Three and a half hours later, with his team in dire straits, Compton returned with stitches in his gashed forehead to play a magnificent innings of 145 not out.

ABOVE RIGHT: Feared Australian fast bowler Ray Lindwall in a peaceful mood on the team ship, sailing towards England, 1948.

Opposing captains Don Bradman and Norman Yardley are snapped by schoolboys with box brownie cameras as they head out to the field for the fourth Test at Headingley.

Watching cricket in England can at times be a tough assignment. Spectators sit through a sudden squall in the second Test at Lord's in 1948.

LEFT: Keith Miller, the 'Errol Flynn of Cricket' … as dashing a player off the field as he was on it.

RIGHT: South African cricketers Eric and Athol Rowan, and captain Dudley Nourse, with springbok mascot, during England's 1948–49 tour of South Africa.

ABOVE: Jim Laker is presented the ball after taking 8–2 for Surrey against Australia in 1950. The England bowler will always be remembered for capturing 19 Australian wickets – 9 for 37 and 10 for 53 – in the Test match at Old Trafford in 1956.

RIGHT: Jim Laker, England's great off spinner at the nets at the Brisbane Cricket Ground in the late 1950s.

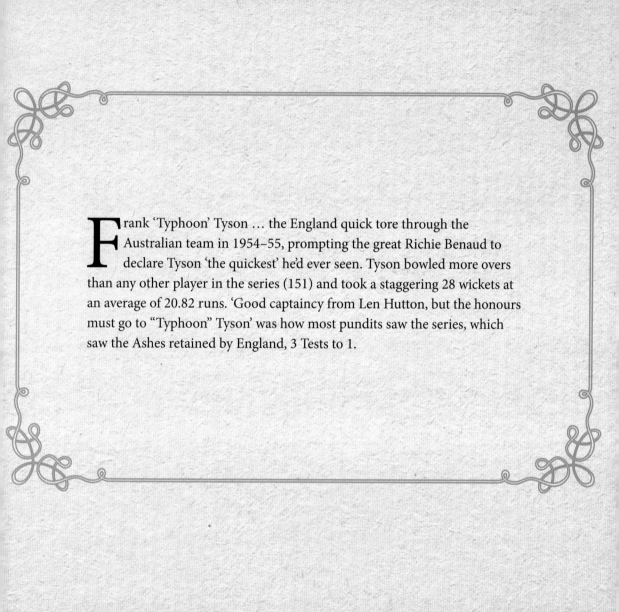

Frank 'Typhoon' Tyson … the England quick tore through the Australian team in 1954–55, prompting the great Richie Benaud to declare Tyson 'the quickest' he'd ever seen. Tyson bowled more overs than any other player in the series (151) and took a staggering 28 wickets at an average of 20.82 runs. 'Good captaincy from Len Hutton, but the honours must go to "Typhoon" Tyson' was how most pundits saw the series, which saw the Ashes retained by England, 3 Tests to 1.

ABOVE: In years gone by, touring squads in England often had a much busier itinerary, with many games against county sides and other commitments visiting local places of interest and official functions. The West Indies team visited the Carr's biscuit factory in Carlisle in 1950 … but how did that kid get in there?

ABOVE LEFT: Players from both teams in the Cumberland and Westmorland v West Indies match played at Edenside, September 1950. Cricket has always been a game that fostered racial integration around the world, both on the field and off it.

BELOW LEFT: Offical function in Carlisle.

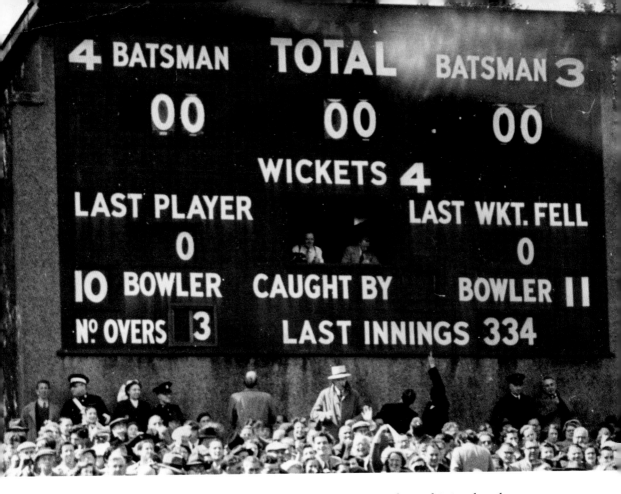

No, the scoreboard attendant has not put up the wrong numbers; this is what the scoreboard looked like after four Indian wickets had fallen without a run having been scored at Leeds in the first Test against England in 1952. Not surprisingly, India eventually lost the match by a large margin.

Australian captain Lindsay Hassett, with his team behind him, makes a farewell speech for the cine-cameras on the deck of the 'Strathaird' at Tilbury as the 1953 Australian cricket team prepares to leave for home.

The occasion is a comic cricket match between the whiskers and the waistcoats. The date was August 1954 when 'Raymond Glendenning, handlebar Moustache Club X1' played against 'Gilbert Harding's Waistcoat Club'. The match was played on Lloyds Sports Ground, Dulwich, in aid of the Star and Garter home, Richmond. In the photo Antony Reynolds (batsman) of the Waistcoat team is seen with Roy Stevens (wicket-keeper) of the Handlebar team and other comical fielders.

"Hindus and Argentines sleep firmly
from twelve to one,
But Mad Dogs and Englishmen
go out in the midday sun."

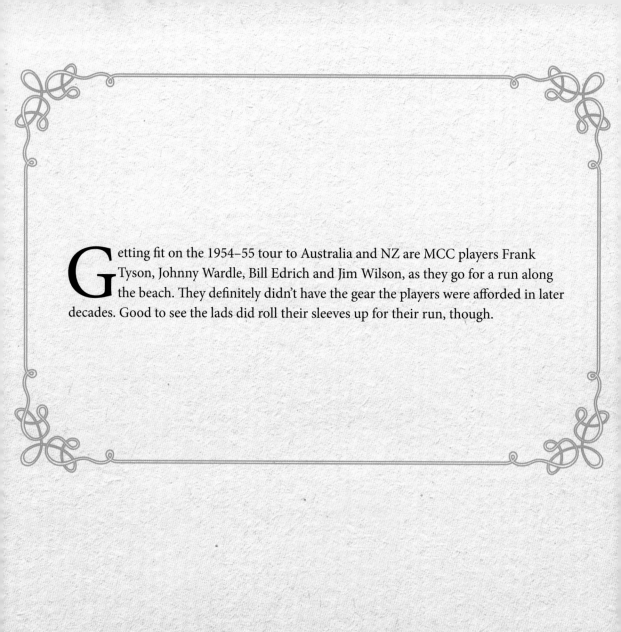

Getting fit on the 1954–55 tour to Australia and NZ are MCC players Frank Tyson, Johnny Wardle, Bill Edrich and Jim Wilson, as they go for a run along the beach. They definitely didn't have the gear the players were afforded in later decades. Good to see the lads did roll their sleeves up for their run, though.

What better way to disperse close in fieldsmen. Here England's Trevor Bailey swings Australian bowler Ian Johnston through the field to the square leg fence as Richie Benaud (left) takes evasive action, December 1954.

Fieldsmen jump for joy as England batsman Tom Graveney is out for a duck, caught by wicket-keeper Langley off Bill Johnston, at the SCG during the second Ashes Test in 1954.

On the slip machine in Perth, October 1954, MCC players Jim Wilson and Len Hutton are watched by curious school boys.

Frank Tyson obliges the junior inhabitants of Yallourn, a Victorian open cut coal centre, with his autograph. He signed over 2,000 autographs before sailing home, spending many hours on board signing photographs, and many hours off the field making Australia's children happy with some 4,000 further signatures. Having helped England to win the Test at Adelaide, Tyson wasn't playing at Yallourn.

The scene at the Adelaide Oval in February 1955, immediately after Godfrey Evans (second from right) had lofted Miller to the square leg boundary and retained the Ashes for England. Two boys are seen rushing Compton (left) for his autograph, three others are battling with the umpire for the stumps and three men (top right) are rushing onto the pitch. The other players are (from left) Keith Miller, Australia's captain Ian Johnson and Arthur Morris.

Joy in the England players' box as Evans scored the winning run to retain the Ashes. From left Alec Bedser, Trevor Bailey, Keith Andrew, Bob Appleyard, Johnny Wardle, Bill Edrich, Frank Tyson (partly hidden), Tom Graveney, Mr J. C. Woodcock of 'The Times,' manager of the England team, Mr C.G. Howard and Colin Cowdrey who seems to be taking in the victory quietly.

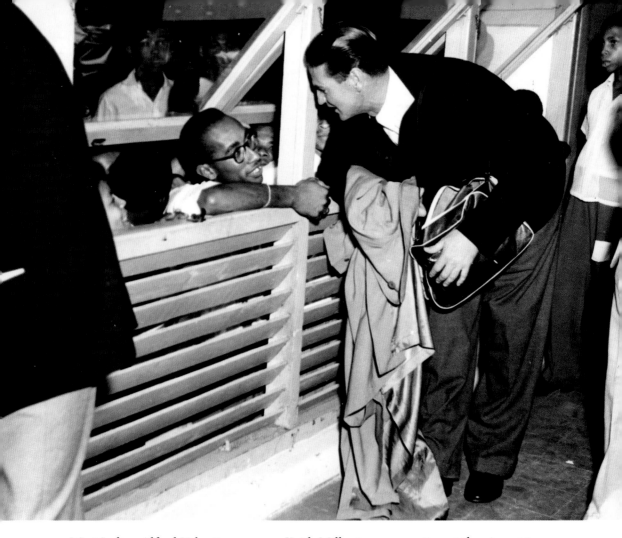

West Indian Alfred Valentine engages Keith Miller in conversation at the airport in 1955. While they competed as hard as always on the field, the comradery off the field was always there too.

Alf Valentine in
Australia in the early
1950s. At the time,
Valentine believed that
the extra rest between
overs didn't make up
for the strain of bowling
eight ball overs.

Australian captain Ian Johnson, in January 1956, 'photobombed' by an interested observer in the background … Sir Don Bradman.

The Duke of Edinburgh, bowling in 1958. Prince Phillip led a team against his Lord Porchester captained opponents in a cricket match held in aid of the National Playing Fields Association, at Highclere Park, Hampshire.

ABOVE LEFT: England fast bowler Fred Trueman carries his gear along Victoria Quay after leaving Iberia in 1958.

ABOVE RIGHT: Veteran New Zealand batsman Bert Sutcliffe puts his hand to his ear after being struck by a bouncer from England fast bowler Freddie Trueman during the first Test at Edgbaston, 1965. Regardless of what the umpire is signalling … the wicket is intact.

Ken Barrington and his teammates stay close together during a bottle-throwing riot in the second Test against the West Indies in Trinidad, 1959–60.

History in the making with the Brisbane Test between Australian and the West Indies in 1960 finishing in a tie, not a draw, for the first time in cricket history.

In early 1961, Melbourne fans gave the West Indian cricketers a farewell unprecedented in world cricket history at the time. Skipper Frank Worrell, riding in an open car with team manager Mr Gerry Gomez, shakes hands with one of the thousands who cheered them on to a civic reception.

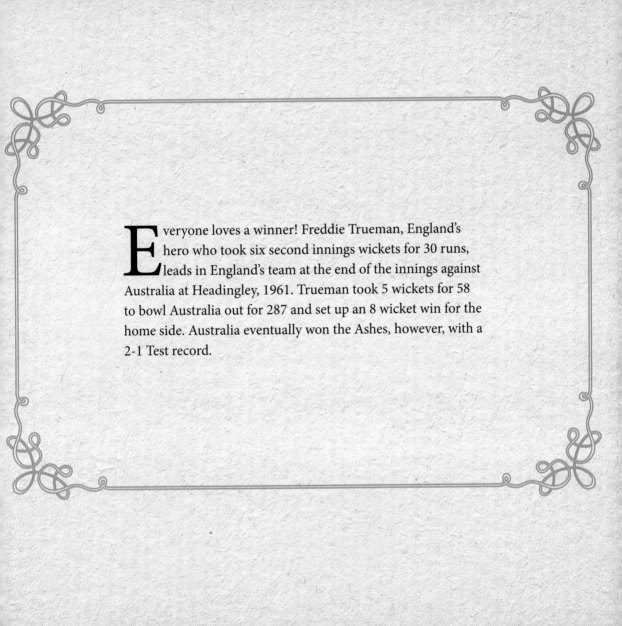

Everyone loves a winner! Freddie Trueman, England's hero who took six second innings wickets for 30 runs, leads in England's team at the end of the innings against Australia at Headingley, 1961. Trueman took 5 wickets for 58 to bowl Australia out for 287 and set up an 8 wicket win for the home side. Australia eventually won the Ashes, however, with a 2-1 Test record.

The West Indian team at Scarborough, 1963. The team includes such greats as Wes Hall, Garry Sobers and Alf Valentine, but what about the little boy in glasses at the end of the line? The lad is clearly channelling Harry Potter – no small feat seeing it is more than three decades before the first book was published – but makes a fashion faux pas of any era by wearing socks and sandals to a sporting match.

West Indian captain Frank Worrell, playing in his last Test, looks around in dismay as he is bowled by England's Brian Statham for 9 during his team's first innings against England in the fifth and final Test at The Oval, August 1963.

West Indian supporters rushing across The Oval following their teams victory in the final Test of the series against England, 1963.

A policeman receives a guard of honour as he carries a bat lost by one of the West Indies batsmen after thousands of spectators swarmed across the pitch after the West Indies victory over England at The Oval, 1963.

Players sprinting to the safety of the pavilion as crowds swarmed onto the pitch after the West Indies had won the final Test and the series against England, 1963.

And its hot tea for the New Zealanders in 1965. Players and umpires enjoying hot tea at a cold and dismal Edgbaston Ground during the morning session, the second day of the first Test against England. The tea was taken out by England twelfth man David Allen (holding teapot). In the centre is England batsman Colin Cowdrey (with cap).

Bobby Simpson, the Australian skipper, walks away from the crease after being caught behind the wicket by keeper Jim Parks, but not before breaking the record for the highest individual score ever at Old Trafford, 311 in 1964. Other players are (bottom left) bowler John Price and (top left) Fred Rumsey. What made this record even more amazing was that it was Simpson's maiden Test century and did not come until his 30th Test for Australia. His century now behind him, Simpson blossomed over his next 32 Tests scoring a further nine centuries.

Former Australian Test captain Lindsay Hassett discovered the fervent female cricketers of Noumea and their equally fervent fans on his way back from the recent English Tests in 1964. 'After the dullness of the English season, it was most refreshing,' he said at the time. He went on to say 'They could certainly give our Australian boys a lesson in enthusiasm.' The women wear uniforms of voluminous, ankle-length 'mother Hubbards' in all colours of the rainbow. They played 17 a side, used rubber balls and homemade bats longer and thinner than the standard Test bat. 'They played on a fairly rough dirt wicket,' said Lindsay, 'but they really hit that ball hard, and they bowl and field well. The whole thing is like a carnival. The barracking is terrific – all in French.'

ABOVE LEFT: The recently retired Richie Benaud threw himself into his post cricket career in various avenues in 1965. Benaud, directing a film on cricket coaching, stands over the camera crew at the Albert Cricket Ground, Melbourne. The film was not shown commercially, but was exhibited at schools.

ABOVE RIGHT: Richie Benaud and his wife Daphne inspecting some of the 'modern' auto-catering equipment they were involved in marketing in the 1960s.

Dressed for the ever-changing English summer weather, or possibly Antarctic conditions, NNC-TV cameramen film the Test match between England and New Zealand at Edgbaston, May 1965.

A line of spectators hold newspapers over their heads to keep off the heavy rain, during the first days play of the second Test between England and the West Indies, June 1966.

The South African Test team arriving at London airport in June 1965. In the front without hats are Peter van der Merwe (captain) and Eddie Barlow (vice-captain).

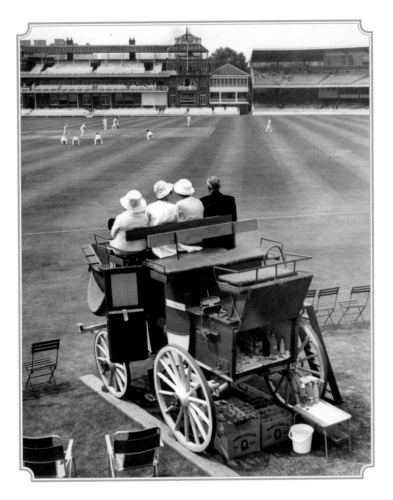

In 1966, spectators at Lord's adopted a slightly different approach for the Eton v Harrow match, enjoying the view on a coach complete with numerous refreshments.

'Tanned by the antipodean sun', members of the MCC arrive at London Airport
in March 1966 after their Australian and New Zealand tour. Left to right are Colin
Cowdrey, Billy Griffiths (tour manager), Mike Smith, Ken Higgs, David Brown and
Geoff Boycott.

Young players gather like seagulls watching the Indians at net practice at Lord's in preparation for the second Test, June 1967.

The iconic Sydney Cricket Ground with names of famous cricketers who have lifted the ball well over the fence for some big hitting sixes. Just some of the great players included are Garfield Sobers, Keith Miller, Victor Trumper, Wally Hammond and Don Bradman.

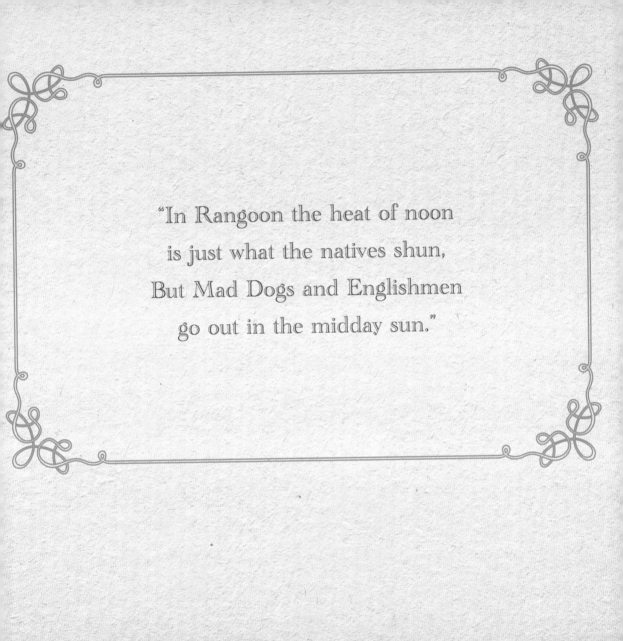

"In Rangoon the heat of noon
is just what the natives shun,
But Mad Dogs and Englishmen
go out in the midday sun."

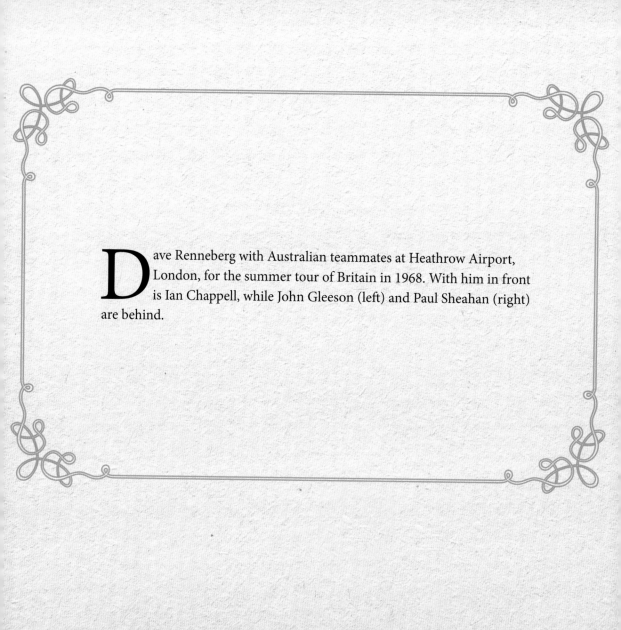

Dave Renneberg with Australian teammates at Heathrow Airport, London, for the summer tour of Britain in 1968. With him in front is Ian Chappell, while John Gleeson (left) and Paul Sheahan (right) are behind.

South African all-rounder Eddie Barlow shows that not everyone had to be an elite athlete to succeed in world cricket. The pugnacious Barlow, nicknamed 'Bunter' after the schoolboy literary character Billy Bunter, scored six Test centuries, was an effective medium pace bowler and as this photo shows, a great slips fielder.

No referral required here with Eddie Barlow, as clean a clean bowled you could imagine. The Rest of the World XI (and South African) batsman was bowled by Salim Altaf for a duck against Pakistan in 1967.

Garry Sobers, the great cricket all-rounder turned film actor, with his name on the chair to prove it. The West Indies Test captain is pictured at Westminster School cricket ground, Vincent Square, London, in May 1968, during the shooting of scenes for 'Two Gentlemen Sharing.' Sobers, making his first appearance in a feature film, is doubling for Hal Frederick, an American actor who plays the part of a Jamaican cricket fanatic.

Australian Cricketer Graham McKenzie looks genuinely happy to be awarded the 1967–68 'Cricketer of the Year Award' even if his trophy looks like it was made in a high school woodshop class.

Much to Alan Knott's excitement, Australian batsman Bob Cowper is brilliantly stumped, as the England keeper whips off the bails off the bowling of Ray Illingworth during the fourth Test at Headingley, 1968.

Come on lads, let's not be shy and I want some nice strong voices! The 1970–71 MCC team who toured Australia and New Zealand singing 'The Ashes Song', composed by Brian Johnston. Most players are getting into the spirit of it, although Bob Willis (centre, back row) clearly wishes he was somewhere else.

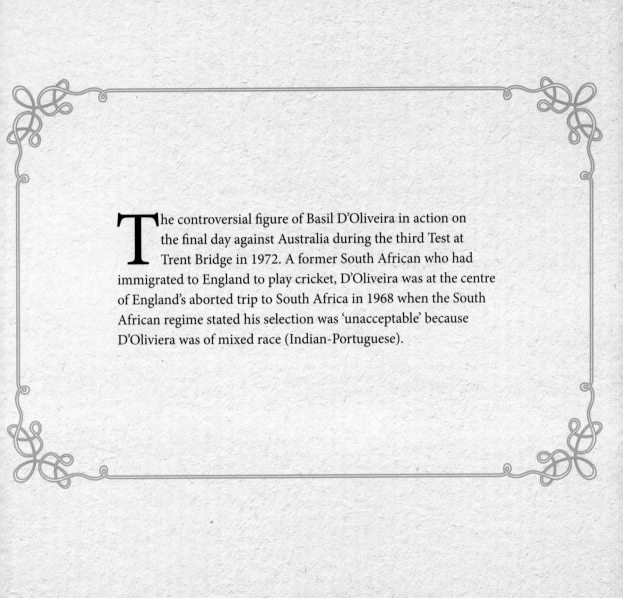

The controversial figure of Basil D'Oliveira in action on the final day against Australia during the third Test at Trent Bridge in 1972. A former South African who had immigrated to England to play cricket, D'Oliveira was at the centre of England's aborted trip to South Africa in 1968 when the South African regime stated his selection was 'unacceptable' because D'Oliviera was of mixed race (Indian-Portuguese).

England bowler John Snow receives a hostile greeting from a spectator late in the day during the final Test match at Sydney in February 1971. This incident occurred shortly after Australian batsman Terry Jenner had been struck on the head by a bouncer from Snow. Beer cans were thrown on to the pitch by the crowd and England captain Ray Illingworth led his team off for a short while.

England's Tony Greig becomes one of 95 batsmen dismissed by the famed combination of 'caught Marsh, bowled Lillee' in Test matches – a record pairing which has yet to be seriously challenged – during the final Test at The Oval in 1972.

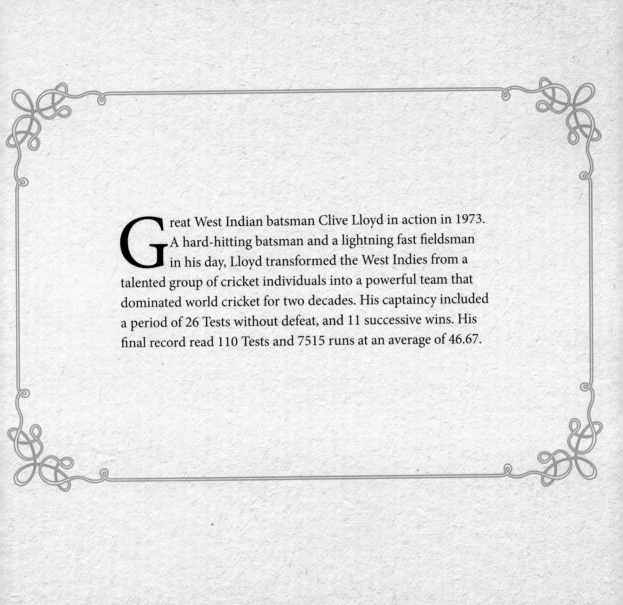

Great West Indian batsman Clive Lloyd in action in 1973. A hard-hitting batsman and a lightning fast fieldsman in his day, Lloyd transformed the West Indies from a talented group of cricket individuals into a powerful team that dominated world cricket for two decades. His captaincy included a period of 26 Tests without defeat, and 11 successive wins. His final record read 110 Tests and 7515 runs at an average of 46.67.

Rohan Kanhai, the West Indies captain, waves to the sea of banner-waving supporters massed in front of the pavilion to acclaim his team after their crushing defeat of England by an innings and 226 runs in the third and final Test match at Lord's, 1973.

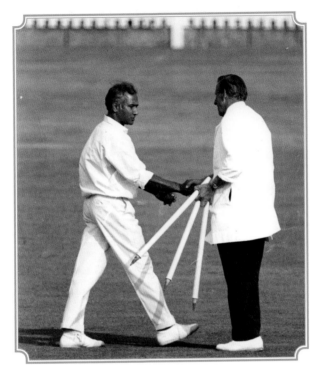

Upon the conclusion of the second Test between England and the West Indies, at Edgbaston, Birmingham 1973, West Indian skipper Rohan Kanhai walked up and shook hands with umpire Arthur Fagg. It signalled the end of any differences between the pair. Earlier in the match, former Kent and England batsman Fagg had threatened to walk out of the match after Kanhai had shown visible dissent when England's Geoff Boycott was given not out. Fagg refused to come out at the beginning of the third day, but was persuaded to resume after one over. Later he had to caution Kanhai over time-wasting by his bowlers.

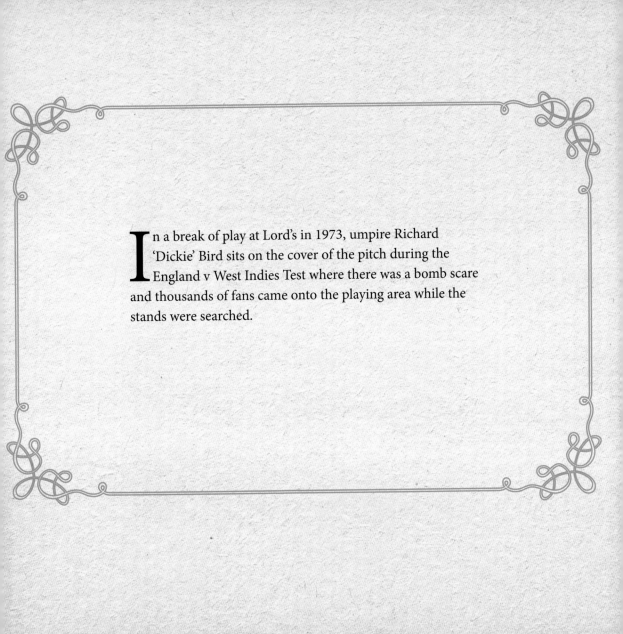

In a break of play at Lord's in 1973, umpire Richard 'Dickie' Bird sits on the cover of the pitch during the England v West Indies Test where there was a bomb scare and thousands of fans came onto the playing area while the stands were searched.

Memo to all touring teams to England from Pakistan's 1971 squad … do not buy identical luggage.

England keeper Alan Knott swatting at flies? Not this talented batsman, who scored five Test centuries and 30 half-tons in his 95 Test career.

Australia's Jeff Thomson's unusual bowling action and his blistering pace made him a terrifying opponent for all batsmen. At the height of his career, and with fellow fast-bowler Dennis Lillee at the other end, they formed one of the most lethal attacks in cricket's history.

England captain Tony
Greig, rugged up to
keep out the April
cold wearing gloves,
three sweaters and a
fur coat before he went
into the nets during a
pre-season workout for
county side Sussex.

West Indies v England, 1981, and it's a frantic scramble as batsmen, fielders, bowler and the umpire grab whatever souvenir they can and get off the pitch before the spectators invasion at the conclusion of the Test.

Tours of the West Indies had its upside, as England players Ian Botham and David Gower show in the Caribbean between matches in 1981. The only down side? Facing those West Indies fast bowlers.

Australia's great fast bowler Dennis Lillee in the fifth Test at Manchester in 1981. Lillee was a magnificent fast bowler, literally the heart and soul of the Australian attack for over a decade. After debuting against England in the Adelaide Test in February 1971, he soon gained world recognition later that year when he decimated a powerful World XI side in Perth, taking 8-29. When he broke down with a spinal stress fracture the following year his career looked over, but a strict training and intensive physiotherapy saw him return to the game at the highest level. His best Test return came against 'the Windies' in 1981, finishing with 7–83 to record a famous upset win for Australia.

Ex-England captain Mike Brearley made a guest appearance dressed as Mahatma Gandhi during the England reception in New Delhi in December 1981. In the background, also in fancy dress, are Graham Dilley and Ian Botham.

Look up the word 'dour' in the Oxford English dictionary and you will see a photo of England opener Geoff Boycott. Boycott scored 22 Test centuries during his international career – a feat spanning 17 years from 1964 to 1981 – and amassed more than 8,000 Test runs at an average of 47.72. But to many of his opponents, especially parochial Australian cricket crowds, watching 'Boycs' bat was akin to watching grass growing in the outfield. But what a frustratingly, steadfast opener he was!

The MCG scoreboard during the Centenary Test match between Australia and England in 1977. A remarkable match that kept the cricket world enthralled for six days, the result went Australia's way, by 45 runs, which just happened to be the same margin in the inaugural Test match played between the two nations a century before.

India's Kapil Dev was regarded as a minor deity by cricket-obsessed fans in his homeland. He could have fielded in a wicker chair if he wanted to, such was his popularity. Here he is, relaxing after a match during presentations.

Charismatic Australian wicketkeeper Rod Marsh in the early 1980s. Nicknamed 'Iron Gloves' by his teammates, Marsh shows the wear and tear on his fingers during a career which netted him 343 Test catches and 12 stumpings in Tests and 120 catches and 4 stumpings in ODI's. Marsh also scored more than 11,000 first class runs … not too shabby at all for a player with fingers like sausages.

The face that scared a thousand batsmen! The one and only Merv Hughes … a big-hearted fast bowler with a mischievous sense of humour and a moustache of large proportions his career showcased his lion hearted determination against all the odds. In the 1988–89 series against the West Indies, Hughes lost bowling partner Geoff Lawson to a broken jaw before finishing with match figures of 13–217 off 73 overs, including a hat trick. On the 1993 Ashes tour, he lost bowling partner Craig McDermott to injury but still took 31 wickets off almost 300 overs over six Tests to help Australia secure a 4–1 series win.

Viv Richards in the West Indies, February 1986. Cricketers didn't come any more talented than Richards, with his front foot mastery, awesome power and brilliant hooking as he rocked back from his front-foot base to hit the ball in front of square. Always a deadly fieldsman who would consistently throw down a wicket from side on, he famously ran out the Chappell brothers, Ian and Greg, and opener Alan Turner in the inaugural World Cup Final in 1975 to secure a West Indies victory. By the time of his retirement, the man with the swagger was revered as the most destructive batsman of his era.

West Indian physio Denis Waight conducts pre-match exercises at Leeds before the opening Test against England in 1991. Ah … the glorious game of cricket! Windmills anyone?

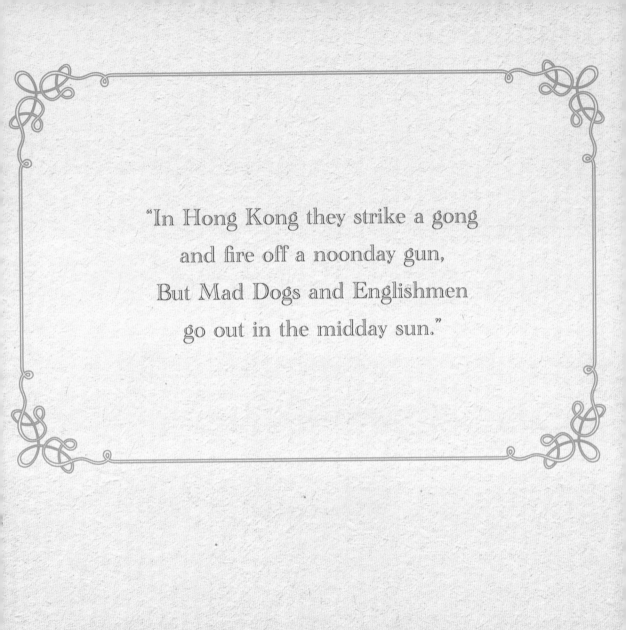

"In Hong Kong they strike a gong
and fire off a noonday gun,
But Mad Dogs and Englishmen
go out in the midday sun."

*I dedicate this book
to Erika & Andrew Collis
and Lara & Ian Greig ... with love*

Author bio:

Ian Collis is a leading authority on sporting history and statistics and is the Head of Stats at Fox Sports, which delivers statistics solutions across all the major sporting codes. Ian also has one of the largest and most diverse collections of memorabilia and sporting photographs. He is also the author of many books including Retro Cricket (2015), Retro Rugby League (2015), Retro Sydney (2013) and Cricket Through the Decades (2012).

A mug celebrating 150 years of the Marylebone Cricket Club (MCC) of England, 1937.

First published in 2015 by New Holland Publishers Pty Ltd
London • Sydney • Auckland

The Chandlery Unit 704 50 Westminster Bridge Road London SE1 7QY United Kingdom
1/66 Gibbes Street Chatswood NSW 2067 Australia
5/39 Woodside Ave Northcote, Auckland 0627 New Zealand

www.newhollandpublishers.com

A record of this book is held at the British Library and the National Library of Australia.

ISBN 9781742578385

Managing Director: Fiona Schultz
Publisher: Alan Whiticker
Project Editor: Jessica McNamara
Designer: Peter Guo
Production Director: Olga Dementiev
Printer: Toppan Leefung Printing Limited

10 9 8 7 6 5 4 3 2 1

Keep up with New Holland Publishers on Facebook
www.facebook.com/NewHollandPublishers